Niall!

 Zayn!

 Liam!

 Harry!

Louis!

Welcome, Superfan!

Niall Horan! Zayn Malik! Liam Payne! Harry Styles! Louis Tomlinson! Five individuals who were brought together by fate, who we all know and love by a different name. They are One Direction, and they are one of the hottest musical groups in the world!

Over the coming pages, we're going to be taking a look at the One Direction story, meeting the boys individually, going over what they've done so far, and getting a taste of what's to come!

So if you're a One Direction Superfan, then pull up a chair, we've got a lot to talk about!

Contents

PULL OUT POSTER!
Head to the middle of this Superfan Guide and you'll find a special poster for you to pull out and stick on your wall!

EDITORIAL
Produced by Loose Fit Media, SBLtd
Art Editor Heather Reeves
Digital Production Manager Nicky Baker

MANAGEMENT
MagBook Publisher Dharmesh Mistry
Operations Director Robin Ryan
MD of Advertising Julian Lloyd-Evans
Newstrade Director David Barker
Commercial & Retail Director Martin Belson
Chief Operating Officer Brett Reynolds
Group Finance Director Ian Leggett
Chief Executive James Tye
Chairman Felix Dennis

MAGBOOK

The MagBook brand is a trademark of Dennis Publishing Ltd. 30 Cleveland St, London W1T 4JD. Company registered in England. All material © Dennis Publishing Ltd, licensed by Felden 2012, and may not be reproduced in whole or part without the consent of the publishers.
The Superfan's Guide to One Direction
ISBN 1-78106-084-3

LICENSING & SYNDICATION
To license this product please contact Carlotta Serantoni on
+44 (0) 20 79076550 or email carlotta_serantoni@dennis.co.uk
To syndicate content from this product please contact Anj Dosaj Halai on
+44(0) 20 7907 6132 or email anj_dosaj-halai@dennis.co.uk

LIABILITY
While every care was taken during the production of this MagBook, the publishers cannot be held responsible for the accuracy of the information or any consequence arising from it. This is not an official publication, and in no way connected with One Direction, Syco Entertainment or Colombia Records. The paper used within this MagBook is produced from sustainable fibre, manufactured by mills with a valid chain of custody.

Pictures Getty Images, Rex Features. Printed at BGP.

The One Dire

It's hard to believe that it's only been two years since One Direction came into our lives. While, individually, Niall, Zayn, Liam, Harry and Louis all had keen musical backgrounds, in the early parts of 2010 they were united by one main thought: entering The X-Factor!

Each of the boys entered the competition separately as solo male artists. None of them knew each other at that stage, and clearly none of them had any idea just how much their world was about to be turned upside-down...

The X-Factor 2010

The 2010 series of The X-Factor – the seventh series since the show started on ITV in the UK – saw each of the five boys put their names forward to audition. As you'd expect, all five of them got past the initial stage of the competition, then they were sent off to the dreaded bootcamp. Things were about to get interesting...

ction Story ♥

How did One Direction come together? To find out, we need to go back to The X-Factor 2010...

Things were a little bit muddled on that particular series of The X-Factor, you might remember. Two of the four judges of The X-Factor – Cheryl Cole and Dannii Minogue – were absent for the bootcamp stage altogether. Eventually Simon Cowell and Louis Walsh were joined by guest judges including Nicole Scherzinger from The Pussycat Dolls. And it would be Ms Scherzinger who was about to play a pivotal part in the formation of One Direction...

Four of the remaining girls joined together to form Belle Amie. They went on to do quite well in the competition, too. They made it through to the live finals and it was only in week four that they finished in the bottom two. When it came to the judge's voting, they were deadlocked (thanks to them being tied with Katie Waisell) but Belle Amie were eliminated as a result of the public vote.

For One Direction, things panned out differently. They too were put together during the show – Niall, Zayn, Liam, Harry and Louis suddenly becoming One Direction! – but they weren't instantly called One Direction. The idea for the name actually came from Harry, who texted it to the other guys. They all liked it and the name was chosen.

But we're jumping ahead of ourselves a bit here. When they were thrown together for the first time, they didn't have a lot of time to work things out. The five boys didn't know each other at all at this stage, remember, and yet they were given five minutes to decide if they wanted to pool their talents into one band. How mad is that?! Given the opportunity in front of them in *The X-Factor*, it's not surprising at all that they all unanimously said yes, though.

Once they'd come together, One Direction progressed nicely and found themselves under the guidance of Simon Cowell himself, who was appointed as their mentor.

Before the live shows began, there was the small matter of getting to know each other. The five had been complete strangers, and now they were together, competing for a massive prize. They've admitted since that these early days weren't quite so easy, with their individual egos clashing a bit!

New Categories

That year's *The X-Factor* was split, as usual, into different categories, but there weren't many strong groups in the competition. It was, therefore, an idea floated by Ms Scherzinger to mix the usual categories up a little. In particular, given the weakness of the groups in the competition, it was suggested that some of the boys and some of the girls who hadn't made the final cut in their original categories be invited to make up groups of their own. It'd happened before on a previous series of the show, but never with quite the same result it was to have here!

Fortunately though, they had a plan. They decided to go off together for two weeks and learn about each other, and to become friends. They went to Harry's house in Cheshire to do that, and by the end of their time there, they were ready to take on whatever *The X-Factor* could throw at them!

The Live Shows

One Direction's first performance together on *The X-Factor*, which they sang at the judges' houses, was *Torn*. Originally recorded by Ednaswap back in 1995, the boys put their own spin on it and progressed through to the live shows as a result.

Not for the first time though, they did have a little bit of trouble on the way. Zayn nearly didn't make it to the final line-up, when a bout of nerves nearly got the better of him. It happened when he was told he had to dance as part of the performance, something that he wasn't keen to do at all. As such, when it came to the performance at boot camp, Zayn stayed backstage.

It was Simon Cowell who intervened. He noticed Zayn wasn't there and went to find out what the problem was. When Zayn eventually told him, Simon managed to persuade him to join the rest of the group, after telling him that he had to change his attitude. And while Zayn didn't give the most comfortable performance in the end, he gave it a try, and the boys managed to progress. Phew!

OMG!
Amazon.com reported in December 2011 that the One Direction calendar was its biggest seller of all time!

From there they continued to impress, week-in, week-out. In week one of the live shows, they sang Coldplay's *Viva La Vida*, comfortably getting through to the next round. Week two? They belted out a version of *My Life Would Suck Without You*, a song originally made famous by Kelly Clarkson (who herself sprung to fame by winning a television singing competition, having won the first ever series of *American Idol* in the USA).

Pink's *Nobody Knows* was their choice for week three of the competition, before wowing the judges again with their rendition of Bonnie Tyler's *Total Eclipse Of The Heart* the week after. By this stage, One Direction were the only group remaining in the competition, as Belle Amie had been knocked out in week four. And they would go right the way through to the final of the show. Not once did the boys end up in the bottom two spaces in the voting, as they impressed the judges and the wider audience with songs such as *Kids In America, Something About The Way You Look Tonight* and *All You Need Is Love*.

With each song, they brought their own charm to it, and the votes kept pouring in for the boys. That said, there wasn't a single week where they were leading the voting. Right throughout the competition, they stayed around the third place mark.

By the time week eight of the competition rolled around, One Direction were singing for a place in the semi-final, and they booked their place

One Direction finish third in The X-Factor.
One Direction's winning single is leaked onto the Internet anyway

Louis is born!

Liam is born!

Harry is born!

December 1991	January 1993	August 1993	September 1993	February 1994	November 2010	December 2010	January 2011

Zayn is born!

Niall is born!

The boys hit number one in the charts for the first time, as part of The X-Factor Finalists' single, Heroes.

One Direction sign up to Simon Cowell's Syco record label

comfortably by singing Bryan Adams' *Summer Of 69* and Joe Cocker's *You Are So Beautiful.*

In the semi-final itself, the pressure was really on, but the boys didn't let it show. They avoided the bottom two once more, singing two songs and winning enough votes to get them through to the big final. Their song choices were Rihanna's *Only Girl (In The World)*, followed by Snow Patrol's *Chasing Cars*. The boys were on after the four other acts, but managed to contain their nerves and sang brilliantly.

The Final

Which led to the big live final, where the One Direction story could have gone off the rails just a little. *The X-Factor* final in 2010 featured four acts: Cher Lloyd, One Direction, Matt Cardle and Rebecca Ferguson.

On the Saturday night show, each act had to perform two songs, with the aim being to avoid elimination and make it through to the grand final on the Sunday. One Direction sang a duet with Robbie Williams as part of the Saturday show, with their two songs that night being Elton John's *Your Song* and Will.i.am's *She's The One.* It was enough to get them through to the Sunday show, as Cher Lloyd was eliminated (although, of course, she'd go on to have a hit single of her own anyway).

Come the Sunday, though, and One Direction got the news that they were dreading: the boys weren't going to be winning *The X-Factor*. In fact, they were the first to be eliminated that night.

That said, finishing in third place in a competition like *The X-Factor* is a fantastic achievement, especially when you consider the tens of thousands of people who enter the show every year. And, as all One Direction fans know, that third place finish was just the beginning!

One Direction: Forever Young is published

What Makes You Beautiful tops the UK singles charts

One Direction's second single, Gotta Be You, is released

The Up All Night Tour begins

Up All Night tops the US Billboard 200 album chart

| February 2011 | July 2011 | September 2011 | November 2011 | December 2011 | January 2012 | March 2012 | February 2013 |

The boys finish recording their first album, Up All Night

One Direction: The Official Annual is published

Their first album, Up All night, is released. Columbia Records sign up One Direction in America

One Thing is released as a promotional single, ahead of its official UK release in February 2012

The One Direction World Tour begins!

They did still manage to leave the show on a high, of course. They sang on that Sunday night the song that had brought them together in the first place, *Torn*, before bowing out, and watching Matt Cardle win the public vote.

For the first time ever on that year's *The X-Factor* it was decided that each of the finalists would record a song of their own. Usually, come the end of the show, each act records the same song and the winner gets their single released. But One Direction had recorded a version of Alphaville's *Forever Young*, and it leaked onto the Internet once the show was over. It seems that the public wasn't ready to write off One Direction just yet, as the song became something of a viral sensation!

What Happened Next?
By the end of December 2010, Niall, Zayn, Liam, Harry and Louis had experienced a life-changing year. But that was to be just the start of it, as a major announcement would land just one month later.

Simon Cowell has been really impressed with One Direction and believed that there was a real gap in the market for a fresh, lively boy band. One Direction very much fitted the bill! As such, it was revealed in January 2011 that he had signed the boys up to his own record label, Syco.

More than that though, Syco really believed in One Direction, and was reported to have invested £2m in the band! Not that it made Niall, Zayn, Liam, Harry and Louis rich, though – according to some reports, they each only saw £8,000 of that £2m. Still, the boys agreed to the deal, and everyone hoped that they would be successful. No-one really had any idea just how successful they were set to become...

The Wait Begins
We still had to wait a while for the fruits of that investment, though. While a book was released in the intervening months to try and quench our thirst for more One Direction, it was the music that fans were waiting for. That said, the book was really good: it was entitled *Forever Young* and, had the boys won *The X-Factor*, it would have been published back in December 2010. As it was, it was released in February 2011, and it was a modified version of the book that would have been released otherwise. It featured lots of lovely pictures of the boys, too!

Single, Album, Tour
The music, though, turned out to be not too far behind, even though it wasn't until September 2011 before we got to properly hear any.

Fortunately, it was well worth the wait! The boys released their debut single, *What Makes You Beautiful*, on 11th September 2011. It had originally been scheduled for release in June, but it was decided to delay it until the new

series of *The X-Factor* started in August. A further delay meant that *What Makes You Beautiful* was eventually released in September.

Fans who had been eagerly awaiting it were quick to snap it up, and *What Makes You Beautiful* shot to the top of the charts. In fact, it didn't just top the charts, it became one of the top 20 best selling singles of the whole year, in spite of the fact that it wasn't released until September.

The single, though, was just a taster of what was to come, as November saw the launch of One Direction's debut album, *Up All Night*. It wasn't just in the UK that it quickly turned into a smash hit, either. *Up All Night* turned out to be a big chart success right across the world, winning the band particularly impressive sales numbers in America and Australia. The boys followed this up quickly with their first tour under their own name (they'd started off 2011 by spending two months out on the road as part of The X-Factor Live Tour). Ticket sales were immense, and One Direction's many fans, us included, had a wonderful time!

2013 promises even more brilliance from One Direction, too. There's already talk of a new album and there's the small matter of the band's first major arena tour. The 2013 One Direction World Tour promises to be absolutely unmissable and, as the boys' success across the world continues to soar, there are many, many great songs and concerts ahead of them.

Long may One Direction reign! **1D**

Niall

Niall James Horan was born in September 1993, and was the youngest of two boys. He was raised in Mullingar, County Westmeath (which is in the Republic Of Ireland) and even in his school days, he was known for his singing. In fact, ==from the age of six, Niall has apparently had a dream that he'd get to the top of the music charts in America.== As it turned out, it was to be more than just a dream...

Niall went to a boys school at first and was soon a member of the school choir, which seemed to keep him busy singing. In fact, as he got older, it wasn't just the choir where he got to show off his vocal talents. ==By the time he got on *The X-Factor*, he'd already been performing quite a lot in Ireland,== and had picked up lots of valuable experience.

He'd also, bizarrely, picked up a real fear of birds. He has something by the name of ornithophobia, which came about when he was on the toilet one day while he was growing up, and he was attacked by a bird! Don't ask us how it happened, but from that point onwards, Niall has always been scared of birds.

The spark that totally ignited his love of music though, was the Christmas when Santa brought the young Niall his first guitar. Even now, Niall refers to it as "the best present I ever received" and from the moment he unwrapped it he played it all the time. ==From the age of eleven, Niall was a very good guitar player.== Santa was clearly clued-up as to the talents of the young man!

Niall's mum and dad divorced when he was just five years old, but they'd noticed his singing talents. It came to prominence during a trip in the car where Niall was singing along and his aunt mentioned that she thought the radio was on! Niall's

Factfile

Full name
Niall James Horan

Birthday
13th September 1993

Born
Mullingar, Ireland

Likes
Michael Buble
Nandos

Im sittin in my room..can hear the fans outside singing "i want" and im high up. they sound good from where i am. haha.. *Niall on Twitter*

OMG!
Niall prefers girls who
don't wear make-up

family have all been firm supporters of his singing. His 81-year-old gran flew to London to watch him in the final of *The X-Factor*!

As word grew about his talent, some people in his hometown used to refer to Niall as the "Irish Justin Bieber", which didn't bother Niall at all. After all, Justin Bieber became famous at a young age through his musical talent, and went on to become one of the biggest music stars in the whole world. There are worse people you could be compared to!

Niall counts a huge array of diverse artists as his musical influences. As well as current recording artists such as Ed Sheeran, Niall has also professed his love for the work of Bon Jovi, Frank Sinatra, Dean Martin, The Eagles and Michael Buble.

Audition Time!

Niall's continuing interest in music led him to the auditions of the 2010 X-Factor competition, although he didn't quite have as smooth a ride as the other boys in the group. For his initial audition, he sang *So Sick*, when the judging panel came to Dublin. Whilst Louis Walsh liked him, the other judges had some reservations about Niall. Louis voted yes, but then Cheryl Cole decided that Niall needed a bit more time to develop, and voted not to take him through to the next round. Simon Cowell decided he was worth giving a chance to, and voted yes, which left the moment of truth in the hands of Katy Perry.

Katy was a guest judge on *The X-Factor*, and she admitted that she shared some concerns with Cheryl as to whether Niall was ready for the competition. Fortunately, though, she decided to side with Louis and Simon, and gave Niall her vote. He

was through the next round, with three out of the four judges voting him through.

At boot camp, he performed his version of Oasis' *Champagne Supernova*, and that was when he hit further problems, as it looked like he was going to leave the competition. But then, you know what happened next... Simon Cowell put him with the other boys, and One Direction was born!

At the time of going to press, Niall isn't in a relationship, and he doesn't seem that enthusiastic about going on too many dates. His idea of a nice night? Just relaxing at home and watching a good movie. If ever he wants someone to watch a movie with, he only has to give us a call! **1D**

OMG!
In his earlier years, Niall played as a support act for Lloyd Daniels during gigs in Dublin

Zayn

One of four children, Zayn Javadd Malik, or Zayn as we know and love him, was born in Bradford back in January 1993. He has an older sister and two younger sisters as well, and he's admitted himself that he was a "handful" as a child, describing his personality as "quite hyperactive". It sounds like his parents had some real headaches with him!

Zayn's father, Yaser, is British Pakistani and his mother, Tricia, is English. His mixed-race background led to some difficulties when he was growing up. People at his first two schools made him feel uncomfortable and were unpleasant about his background, but eventually he managed to settle at Tong High School. From there, he discovered his musical talent and he could put that hyperactivity to better use!

He also became more and more popular at his new school, and he says that it was when he became a teenager that he began to take more and more time over how he looked. He's admitted that he got a bit obsessed with his hair, too, waking up well before his sister so he could spend time getting it right! It didn't always go to plan, though, and Zayn has been honest about the fact that not every haircut he had was a brilliant one.

In the past, Zayn has also admitted that he used to be really, really shy, and it's only really his time in One Direction that has changed that. Now, he says that he finds it a lot easier to talk to people.

Still, in spite of that shyness, Zayn has always been a singer and, perhaps inevitably, he was part of the choir at his primary school. One day, they all sang together in his local Asda store, too. We bet the shoppers there had no idea that they were getting a very early glimpse of a superstar!

Factfile

Full name
Zayn Javadd Malik

Birthday
12th January 1993

Born
Bradford

Likes
Comic books
Drawing

In life we always fall for the person that will never fall for us always want something that we can't and always say things we shouldn't :s *Zayn on Twitter*

21

OMG!
When they were on The X-Factor together, Justin Bieber offered to help Zayn with his dancing! Wow!

It was to be just the start of his singing career, though, and, as you all know, much greater things were on the horizon...

The Audition

It was while he was at Tong High School that Zayn made the life-changing decision to audition for *The X-Factor*. But the first time around, things didn't exactly go to plan. As Zayn himself has admitted, the first time he went to audition for the show, in 2009, his nervousness won out, and he fumbled his chance. Being nervous would, of course, come back to haunt Zayn, but fortunately, he was able to get the better of it.

His failed audition in 2009 made him more determined than ever to succeed when he decided to enter the show again the year after. He still got nervous, but this time, it was encouragement from his mum that seemed to make the difference. This time, he was 17 years old, and the audition would ultimately change his life.

His audition song, when he went along for the Manchester leg of the try-outs back in 2010, was *You Should Let Me Love You*, by Mario. Given his tendency for nervousness, Zayn did a remarkable job and really impressed the judges!

Mind you, those of us watching *The X-Factor* wouldn't have known all this at the time. That's because Zayn's audition wasn't broadcast as part of the main show, and we only got to see it properly for the first time on *The Xtra Factor*. Still, it was worth the wait!

And, importantly, just because he didn't make the main show at first, it didn't mean he hadn't impressed the judges. As it happened, Zayn's audition won three "Yes" votes from Simon Cowell, Nicole Scherzinger and Louis Walsh. He was through to the next round, with everyone impressed by his vocal talent.

He entered the category for the boys and made some progress in the show before fate took hold and he was eventually invited to join One Direction. From that point onwards, his life was never going to be the same!

Relationships

Zayn hit the headlines at one stage due to his relationship with Rebecca Ferguson. Rebecca was also a contestant on *The X-Factor* back in 2010 and she eventually finished second in the show, one place ahead of One Direction. She and Zayn split up after a few months though: the fact that Rebecca was six years older than Zayn presumably didn't help!

Zayn has also dated another *X-Factor* contestant, though. At one stage he was involved with Geneva Lane, although that too didn't last too long either.

More recently, Zayn has been spending time – when he can find a moment in his schedule! – with Perrie Edwards. Perrie is part of the band Little Mix who won *The X-Factor* in 2011. **1D**

23

OMG!
Liam has 11 GCSEs,
the clever clogs!

Liam

Life wasn't easy for Liam in his early years. That's because he was born three weeks early and, as a result of that, he had to battle with quite a lot of health problems when he was growing up.

He was born in Wolverhampton and is the youngest of three children (he has two older sisters). Particularly in the first three to four years of his life though, Liam had to spend quite a lot of time in hospital undergoing lots of tests and getting help dealing with the strange pain that he was suffering. It got so bad at one point that he had to have 32 injections in his arm, twice a day, just to keep on top of the pain he was going through. Ouch!

His doctors eventually noticed that he had a problem with one of his kidneys, and that's something that Liam has learned to live with ever since. Only one of his kidneys works properly, so you won't find Liam drinking alcohol or anything like that!

Early Years

Growing up, Liam himself admitted that he was the "naughty boy" at his local school. He didn't have the best of times, either. He was bullied at school for a time, but he turned to sport to help himself get through it. And it turns out that Liam was quite the sporty type!

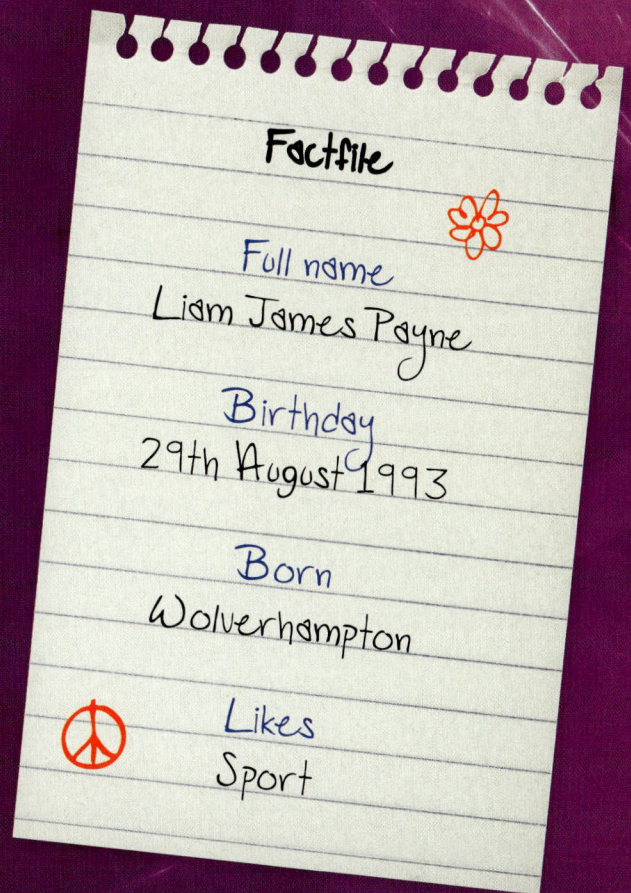

He discovered, for instance, that he was a really good cross-country runner, which sounds like a lot of hard work to us. He used to get up at five o'clock in the morning just to go for a run and get more practise in! It was worth it though, because he got so good at it he was put in his school's under-18 cross country team. The thing is, Liam was only 12 years old at the time. That's how fast he was!

It wasn't just running that he was into, either. Liam also took up boxing as a way to help him deal with the people who were bullying him. He said that it was boxing that helped him build his confidence. And, fortunately, he proved to have confidence in his music, too!

So excited for this arena tour 2013 ahhhh its gunna be amazing this ones for u guys and we hope u enjoy it woohoooo :) *Liam on Twitter*

Initially, music wasn't where Liam's ambitions lay though. Most of all, he wanted to be an Olympic athlete. What stopped him pursuing sport instead of music though, was the disappointment he faced when he was 14. He only just missed out on winning a place in the England schools running team and, when that happened, he decided to focus on his singing instead.

Singing wasn't new to Liam, though. Even when he was six years old, he'd proven that he was a good singer and was regularly entertaining his family and taking part in karaoke. When he was 12 he joined up with a group called Pink Productions that put on performing arts shows.

Music

When he finished school, Liam went to the City Of Wolverhampton College, near where he lived, and took a music technology course. But even before he'd done that, he'd had his first brush with *The X-Factor*!

Unlike the other boys, Liam had got onto *The X-Factor* before, when he was just 14 years old. He auditioned successfully back in 2008, and he sailed through the auditions and boot camp, eventually getting to the stage of the programme where he had to go the judges' houses. In his case, he had to go to the home of Simon Cowell, and it was there that Simon gave him the bad news: he wouldn't be going any further in the competition!

Simon's reasoning was that Liam was simply too young for it, which does beg the question why they let him get so far in the first place! But Simon did have some important advice for Liam, which was to prove vital. He said to Liam that he should come back again in two years time and try again. And that's just what

Liam did. In fact, he would have auditioned again in 2009, but the rules changed, which meant you needed to be at least 16 years old to take part.

When he auditioned for the show a second time, in 2010, Liam was now 16 years old. And he performed a song for his audition by one of his big influences: Justin Timberlake. Liam's rendition of Cry Me A River brought the house down, and the judges were really impressed. They put him through to the next round.

Liam did, of course, have to face some more disappointment when he got to the boot camp stage of the competition, as he was rejected again. But then came the suggestion that he should join the other four boys in One Direction and, all of a sudden, Liam had his big break!

Liam is another one of the boys who met his girlfriend while on *The X-Factor*. He struck up a relationship with one of the backing dancers on the show, Danielle Peazer (who has danced for Jessie J and The Saturdays!) and they've stayed together since 2010. Not that it's always been easy: lots of people have sent nasty messages regarding Danielle and Liam is understandably very protective of her. All the nastiness is showing little sign of driving Liam and Danielle apart.

Still in his teens, it's amazing how much Liam has had to battle through to get to where he is today. He's clever, he's hot, and he can sing brilliantly. And One Direction just wouldn't be the same without him! **1D**

Harry

Harry is the youngest member of One Direction, having been born on 1st February 1994. He's one of two children and he has an elder sister. When he was young he went to live in the village of Holmes Chapel in Cheshire and he went to the Holmes Chapel Comprehensive School.

Like many of the boys, Harry didn't have the easiest time growing up. His parents divorced when he was seven years old, and he's since described it as a "weird time" where he didn't really understand quite what was going on.

Things did settle down for Harry in the end, though, and he was soon getting passionate about his music. He always loved singing, and he was actually in a band a long time before One Direction came about. The band was called White Eskimo. And, naturally, Harry was its lead singer.

White Eskimo had a bit of success, too, with the group winning a local Battle Of The Bands competition and earning themselves a few fans as they did so. For Harry, too, he knew then that he really enjoyed performing his music in front of a big crowd of people and he might just have worked out that he was good at it, too! We'd certainly have loved seeing White Eskimo perform. You can see some examples of their music on YouTube!

OMG!
Harry has four nipples!

Factfile

Full name
Harry Edward Styles

Birthday
1st February 1994

Born
Evesham

Likes
The Beatles

I watched The Lion King on the plane... and I genuinely think it's one of the best films ever made. *Harry on Twitter*

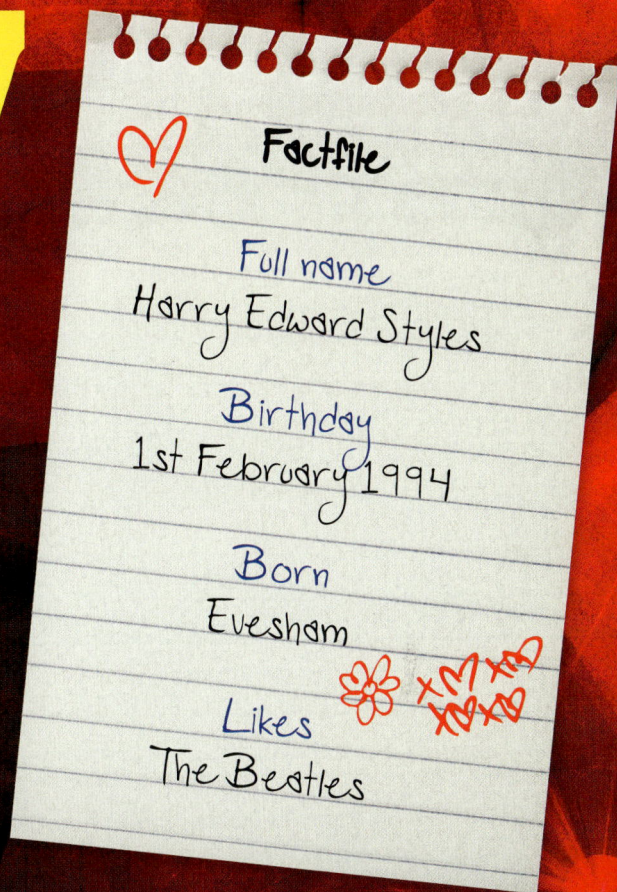

29

Amongst the early influences that Harry has talked about is Elvis Presley. He also very strongly remembers that his dad would play him the music of The Beatles as he was growing up, and he says he still listens to their music a lot. That said, Harry has a wide range of music that he loves, including work by the likes of Coldplay and Kings Of Leon. We'd love to see what he's got on his iPod. We bet it's almost full!

The X-Factor

His continual passion for music eventually led to Harry's very wise decision to audition for *The X-Factor*. The main reason that Harry wanted to take part in the show is that he wanted someone else to give an opinion on his singing. His mum had continually tried to tell him what a good singer he was, but he wanted to find out if other people felt the same way. Yes, Harry, they did!

He stepped up for the 2010 competition, and went before the dreaded panel of judges, singing *Isn't She Lovely*. But not everyone was impressed with Harry's audition. Louis Walsh in particular had concerns over whether Harry was right for the competition, and whether he would do well in it going forward. Fortunately though, not everyone agreed with Louis (does anyone ever?!), and Harry got the votes he needed to get to boot camp!

When he got to boot camp, Harry was – along with the other four boys – rejected at first for the next stage of the competition. The judges hadn't been impressed enough with his version of *Stop Crying Your Heart Out* and initially decided not to put him through. As a solo performer, his *X-Factor* journey was over. But as a band member? It was only just beginning!

It was Harry who came up with the name for the band, deciding on One Direction because he reckoned that it would sound really good when it was read out by the announcer on *The X-Factor*. And we think Harry got that one right! He texted his idea for the name to the other members of the group, and they all quickly agreed too. One Direction was officially born, there and then!

Harry got into a bit of bother on *The X-Factor* final due to a comment he apparently whispered to the eventual winner, Matt Cardle, after the result was announced. It was a bit rude, but Harry apparently suggested something along the lines that Matt wouldn't have much trouble getting girlfriends in the future. In the end, the exact comment was never confirmed, and everyone seemed to laugh it off.

Since he shot to fame with One Direction, Harry has moved in with Louis Tomlinson, and the two of them share a flat together. Harry also dated, but not for very long, Caroline Flack. This caused lots of things to be written about them both in the media, as Caroline Flack, a television presenter and host of *The Xtra Factor*, is 15 years older than Harry! The two of them eventually split up, but they remain good friends. 1D

OMG!
Harry says he would be a loyal boyfriend!

OMG!

Did you know that one of Louis' biggest influences is Robbie Williams? That explains why he was so pleased to meet him on The X-Factor!

Louis

Given that Louis spends a lot of time surrounded by girls, it's perhaps a good job that he grew up alongside sisters. He said that he always wanted a brother when he was growing up, but Louis was actually the eldest of five children and the only male sibling. He has four younger sisters, two of whom are twins – we bet his house was quiet!

Louis isn't just the eldest of five children though, he's also the eldest of the five members of One Direction! He was born on Christmas Eve – we wonder if he still gets two lots of presents?! – back in 1991, although his mum and dad split up when he was still young.

Louis went to school at The Hayfield School, but it was when he joined the sixth form of Hall Cross School that things really started to happen for him. Even though his musical talent had been obvious for some time beforehand, it was when he took part in a number of musical productions during his time at Hall Cross that it became obvious he had something really special.

One role that really did help Louis on his path to fame was getting the lead in a production of *Grease*. The singing and dancing he had to do there certainly held him in good stead for the future. He'd be doing that a lot more on stage in the years to come...

Mind you, he did struggle at Hall Cross for a while. He admitted that he didn't do too much work during his first year there, as he was out and about for a lot of the time. Too much partying and not enough work meant that he failed the first year of his A levels. Oh dear! He decided in the end to go back to Hall Cross and start them all again.

By this time though, Louis had done some professional acting work and clearly had been bitten by the performance bug. For instance, he appeared as an extra on the TV show *Fat Friends* and then landed small roles in a couple of others: He appeared in an ITV

Little unknown fact I'm 1/16 Belgian *Louis on Twitter*

33

drama by the name of *If I Had You* and the BBC's school-based drama *Waterloo Road* also found work for him.

Auditions

Presumably fuelled by his love for performance, Louis eventually decided to audition for *The X-Factor*, so he turned up to the 2010 try-outs. He chose *Hey There Delilah* as his song and his voice quickly impressed the judges. All three judges that he sang before said "Yes" to him and Louis sailed through to the next round of the competition.

As with the rest of the boys, Louis' *X-Factor* journey threatened to end at boot camp. He'd sung *Make You Feel My Love*, but it wasn't enough to convince the judges to instantly let him through to the next stage of the competition. Instead, he was brought together as part of the plan to give the world One Direction. And a rather brilliant plan it's turned out to be!

Not that Louis and the boys found it easy. As he's pointed out, the five of them didn't know each and they were only given five minutes together in a room to decide whether they wanted to join together as a band or not. Fortunately, they did. "There was no question", admitted Louis afterwards.

OMG!
Did you know that, when they were babies, Louis' twin sisters were used as extras on the TV show Fat Friends?

From the judges' houses onwards, One Direction sailed through the competition. There was a slight hitch along the way: when One Direction went to Simon Cowell's house, Louis had to be taken to hospital when he cut his foot on a sea urchin! That cut into the band's rehearsal time and made things just a little bit more stressful, but they coped brilliantly well.

These days? Louis is not only a member of the hottest boy band on the planet (and he's apparently the practical joker amongst the five) but he also gets to share a flat with his band mate, Harry Styles. He's also in a relationship with a student, Eleanor Calder, and the two of them have been together since the end of 2011. **1D**

OMG!
Louis loves the TV show Britain's Got Talent

Singles

What Makes You Beautiful

First radio play:	10th August 2011
First release:	11th September 2011
UK chart position:	1
Running time:	3 minutes 22 seconds

It was nine months after they'd finished in third place on The X-Factor that One Direction finally released their debut single – and a very special single it turned out to be!

The song was written by Rami Yacoub, Carl Falk and Savan Kotecha, and was deliberately picked for being a fast, bright pop song. After they had signed up to Simon Cowell's Syco Music at the start of 2011, they set to work on the song straight away, eventually heading off to Stockholm in Sweden to record it. The band have said that once they'd put the song together, they knew they wanted it to be their debut single!

There'd still be a bit of a wait for its release, though. *What Makes You Beautiful* was kept under covers until 10th August 2011, when it got its very first public airing. It debuted on BBC Radio 1, and the single itself was then released just over a month later, on 11th September 2011.

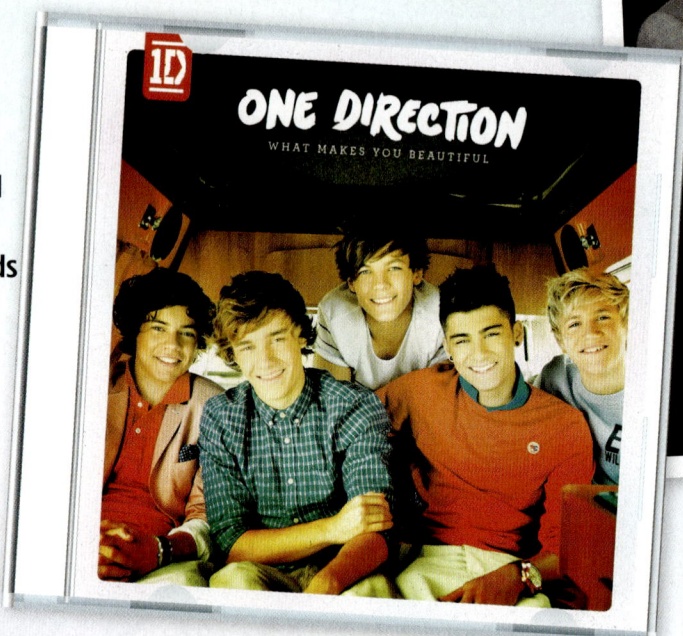

One Direction

The catchiness of the song was instantly praised and, by the time the release date came around, it was already a guaranteed hit. No other single ever on the Sony label, of which Syco was a part, had attracted so many pre-orders. It came as little surprise in the end when, in its first week, the single sold an incredible 153,965 copies. Over half a million copies of *What Makes You Beautiful* have now been sold in Britain alone!

It's not just been a British hit, though. *What Makes You Beautiful* has also been a success right around the world. It broke into the top ten in Australia, Canada, Belgium, Mexico, New Zealand, Poland and, of course, America. Even the B-side to the record, *Na Na Na*, broke into the charts of its own accord in both Ireland and Australia.

The success for *What Makes You Beautiful* was ultimately crowned at the 2012 Brit Awards, where One Direction deservedly took home the prize for Best British Single.

Our Rating ♡ ♡ ♡ ♡ ♡

The X-Factor Singles

As well as the singles they released on their own, One Direction have also appeared on two singles related to the X-Factor. The first was put out by The X-Factor finalists, and was called Heroes. That went to number one. As did the one they recorded the year after, Wishing On A Star. This also featured that year's X-Factor finalists, but both One Direction and JLS were invited back to be included on the record, too. Both were charity singles.

Gotta Be You

First release: 11th November 2011
UK chart position: 3
Running time: 4 minutes 5 seconds

Following on from the success of *What Makes You Beautiful* was no small feat, not least because it was still in the charts by the time One Direction came to release their second single. *Gotta Be You*, though, while not as successful, turned out to be another big hit for the band.

Its release was announced the month after the release of *What Makes You Beautiful*. *Gotta Be You* has a different feel to their debut single, and this time it was written by August Rigo and Steve Mac. The big day: 11th November 2011, exactly two months after the release of *What Makes You Beautiful*.

The band unveiled the cover image for *Gotta Be You* in October and performed it live on television for the first time on *The X-Factor*. They debuted it on one of the Sunday night results shows – on 13th November to be exact – and also performed the song later in the week as part of the BBC's Children In Need.

Given that it was a second single, the release of *Gotta Be You* wasn't as wide, but it was still rolled out in both the UK and Ireland. At one stage, it looked as though it as going to top the UK charts in the week of its release, but eventually the boys had to settle for third place! In its first week, it sold just short of 60,000 copies in Britain.

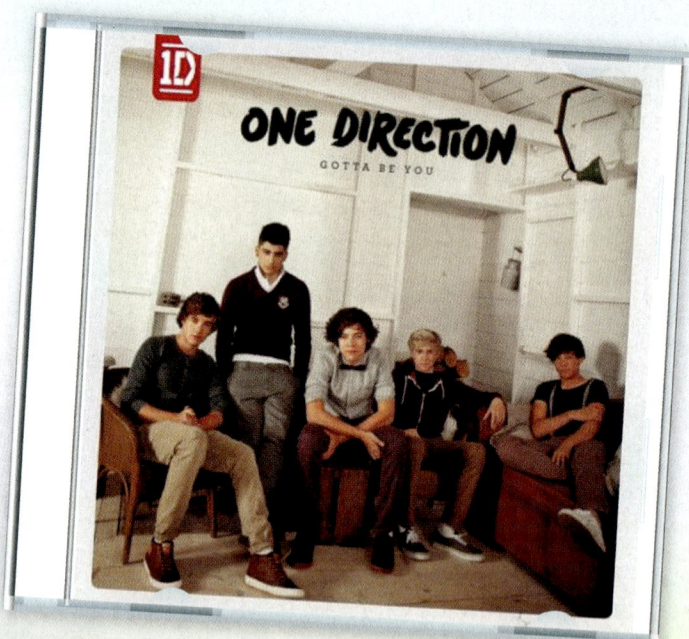

At the time of writing, the single hasn't been released anywhere outside of the UK and Ireland, apart from its appearance on the *Up All Night* album. There are two remixes, and a slightly different American version of the song, both of which are well worth checking out!

Our Rating ♡ ♡ ♡ ♡

One Thing

First release: 6th January 2012
UK chart position: 9
Running time: 3 minutes 10 seconds

The boys scored a third British top ten hit with the release of their third single *One Thing*, which again features on the *Up All Night* album. As with *What Makes You Beautiful*, *One Thing* was written by Rami Yacoub, Carl Falk and Savan Kotecha and, at first, it was used as a promotional single in some countries around Europe.

It got a single release of its own in the UK though, coming out on 12th February 2012. Amazingly, it shot to number nine in the charts. Given that the song had already featured on a massive hit album, that's an incredible feat, and the boys thoroughly deserved it!

The single was quite widely released around the world, too, enjoying particular success in Hungary (where it reached number four in the singles charts), Australia (number three) and Ireland (number six). Oddly, the UK was the last country that the single was released in, having been rolled out in ten others at the start of January!

Even more oddly, even though the song wasn't actually released as a single in either America and Canada, it still managed to break into the singles chart in both those countries. This was off the back of its download sales, with *One Thing* getting to number 62 in the American Billboard Hot 100!

The band performed *One Thing* live in front of an audience for the first time in December 2011, when they appeared at the O2 Arena in London, for Capital FM's Jingle Bell Ball. And the week before it came out in the UK, One Direction appeared on *Dancing On Ice* to sing it, too. The band caused something of a furore when they appeared on the *Today Show* in America, with over 10,000 fans desperate to see their heroes in the flesh!

Our Rating ♡ ♡ ♡ ♡

UP ALL NIGHT

One Direction's first album!

Considering it was December 2010 that One Direction finished third in *The X-Factor*, it took some time after that for their debut album to come together. Of course, you can hardly expect them to make a record overnight (especially one as brilliant as the one we got!) but us fans were desperate to hear just what the boys would come up with next! Still, given that *X-Factor* winners generally have to wait a year before their album is released, having to wait just nine months suddenly doesn't seem quite so bad.

The Announcement

It was eventually announced, after the boys were signed to Simon Cowell's Syco recording label, that One Direction would release their first album in the second half of 2011. And some

The Superfan's guide to
One Direction

BIG TIME

BIG TIME
MOVIE

nickelodeon

nickelode

BIG TI
MOVI

nickelode

The Superfan's guide to
One Direction

accomplished songwriters were brought on board to help pen the tunes. Amongst those who contributed work were Kelly Clarkson and Ed Sheeran, and the music was eventually recorded in England, America and Sweden.

For a while, the release was still shrouded in some mystery. It wasn't clear exactly when the album would be available for sale, what it would be called, or what would be on it. Things looked like they were moving forward when the boys announced in April 2011 that the lead song from the album was set to be *What Makes You Beautiful* (we love that song so much!) and that it was going to be released in June. That got our hopes up: we thought the album would be a few

weeks after that. However, the single got pushed all the way back to September, when it eventually went on sale.

We were still none-the-wiser as to the release date of the album itself...

The answers to our questions started to filter through in October 2011. The boys put up a special challenge on their official website and, once it was completed, the cover of the album and the name of the album would be revealed to the eagerly awaiting world!

You'll be surprised to hear that it didn't take long to complete the challenge, and that's when we found out for the first time that the album would go by the name of Up All Night. By then we also knew that it was just a month away from release, with Up All Night making its official debut on 18th November 2011. What a great day that was!

The Release

The wait was certainly worth it. Even the stuffiest of critics seemed to like the album, and us fans absolutely loved it! And the great news was that it flew off shop shelves at breakneck speed.

In its first week on sale in the UK, Up All Night sold a massive 138,631 copies! It entered the UK Album Chart at number two, finishing in second place to Rihanna's Talk That Talk. And from that point onward, Up All Night has continued to sell. Over 500,000 copies of it have sold in the UK alone. Britain has very, very good taste!

But the success of the album didn't stop there. It topped the album charts in Canada, Croatia, Australia, Italy, Mexico, New Zealand and Sweden. It also hit the top ten of the albums chart in Belgium, Denmark, Holland, Finland, Hungary, Ireland, Poland, Portugal, Scotland, Spain and Taiwan!

Up All Night didn't make it to number one in the UK, sadly, but it sold more copies than any other second-placed album that year, so that's a big achievement in itself.

Plus, had it been released even earlier in the year, then it would easily have been one of the top ten selling albums of 2011 in the UK. As it was, in just six weeks it made it to the number 16 spot. That's an incredible achievement, especially for a debut album. And it's an album that's kept selling well into 2012, too.

The Success

But the Up All Night journey was a long way from being done. It's very,

very hard for any group to break the American charts, but that's just what One Direction managed to do next. In its first week of release, off the back of a clever promotional campaign that had been running for four months *Up All Night* went straight to the top of the American Billboard 200 chart! The album sold 176,000 copies in just one week and One Direction became the first British group to ever go to number one in the Billboard 200 with their very first album. We'd guess it'll be a very long time before anyone manages it again.

Up All Night isn't just an amazing album, it's also an amazingly successful one. Just think, when the five boys were given five minutes to decide if they wanted to be in a group together, could they ever have imagined they would go on to such worldwide success? It's incredible to think that from one moment on *The X-Factor*, such a record-breaking, brilliant album should appear.

We're so glad it did, and we can't wait to hear what the boys come up with for their second album. We bet it'll be brilliant, and we hope we don't have to wait anywhere near as long to hear it this time round. Fingers crossed! **1D**

Critic Reviews

"Up All Night marches to a new, postmillennial tiger beat: The irresistibly bouncy "One Thing," the Kelly Clarkson-co-penned "Tell Me a Lie," and the party-till-Mom-comes-home title track are all charmingly gimmick-free slices of white-bread wonder"
Entertainment Weekly

"The boys' debut album, Up All Night, is a little bit of a revelation"
Popmatters

"As a starting point for One Direction fan memorabilia, for which it appears there is limitless potential for the time being, this is a perfectly sized, and targeted, collection."
All Music

One Direction

The X-Factor Tour 2011

If we're totally honest, the first live tour the One Direction boys did together didn't make the best use of their talents. It came as part of The X-Factor Live Tour in 2011, which played 47 shows between February and April. One Direction were one part of a line-up that also included the show's winner, Matt Cardle, as well as acts such as Cher Lloyd, Wagner (one or two members of One Direction don't get on with him at all!) Rebecca Ferguson and Katie Waissel.

The X-Factor Live Tour 2011 setlist

One Direction only got a couple of songs at The X-Factor Live Tour 2011, and they were...

Only Girl (In The World)
Chasing Cars
Kids In America
My Life Would Suck Without You
Forever Young

And then the boys joined the rest of the finalists to sing Heroes.

The boys weren't singing their own material at this stage, but you didn't need to be asked twice who were the stars of the night. Wherever The X-Factor tour went, it was One Direction who were getting the loudest cheers!

The boys did well on the tour, too, but only had a few songs to showcase their talents. It would all prove to be a useful practise run for what was to follow later in the year, when One Direction went on tour as the headline act for the very first time...

The Up All Night Tour
2011-2012

If it took some time for One Direction to launch their first single, *What Makes You Beautiful*, thank goodness it wasn't too long after that the boys confirmed they'd be taking their music back out on the road!

The Up All Night Tour was announced very shortly after, kicking off on 18th December 2011. The tour would take the boys across the UK first, ending up in Belfast at the end of January 2012. After that, One Direction had a few months off from touring, before resuming Up All Night in Australia, in April 2012.

By the end of May, they were on the road in America and Canada, with the Up All Night Tour finally coming to an end on 1st July 2012. The last gig was played in Sunrise, in the United States.

It goes without saying that the tour was a gigantic, massive success. Tickets for

1 Na Na Na
2 Stand Up
3 I Wish
4 I Gotta Feeling
5 Stereo Hearts
6 Valerie
7 Torn
8 Moments
9 Up All Night
10 More Than This
11 Tell Me A Lie
12 Everything About You
13 Use Somebody
14 One Thing
15 Save You Tonight
16 What Makes You Beautiful

And then, for an encore, the boys sang I Want.

the British shows in particular were gone in some cases in less than a minute! In Australia, the shows in several venues took less than ten minutes to sell out, and the same happened again in the USA. Lots of people want to see One Direction doing what they do best, and who can blame them?

The tour was also recorded for a DVD release. The show chosen was the Bournemouth date at the start of January 2012. It's a great souvenir of an amazing tour. In all, the boys performed 62 concerts and each and every one of them was just superb!

The 2013 World Tour

2013 is a massive year for One Direction, with the boys embarking on a massive world tour that will take their music to all corners of the globe. Over 85 concerts are going to be played as part of the tour, which will take them right around the UK first, before heading off to America, Canada, Australia and New Zealand.

The tour was officially revealed at the 2012 Brit Awards, when One Direction had just picked up a prize for Best British Single. Liam took to the microphone as part of the boys' acceptance speeches and thanked the team who work so hard for the band, revealing that "we're going to be doing our own arena tour".

And what an arena tour! The start date has been confirmed for 22nd February 2013, with the boys touring through until October. They might even announce more gigs, too! Given how quickly the tickets have sold, the boys have kept having to lay on extra shows, that's how popular they are!

And they still can't keep up with demand. Fans right around the world have been begging for tickets, with the Australia and New Zealand leg of the tour alone bringing in around £10m in ticket sales, with 190,000 sold! When they hit America, too, they get to play the legendary Madison Square Garden – how cool is that?! **1D**

The Best One Direc

Up All Night Live Concert DVD
£8.99

It's not as good as being at one of the gigs, obviously, but it's about the next best thing! The Up All Night Concert DVD caught the boys on their tour, capturing their amazing gig at Bournemouth's BIC Arena in January 2012! As well as hearing them sing their best songs, the DVD also includes a chance to go behind the scenes with a documentary that follows them on their tour. You also get music videos for *What Makes You Beautiful, Gotta Be You* and *One Thing*!

Here are some of the things that no true One Direction fan can be without!

The Tour Programme
£9.99

Packed with pictures of Harry, Zayn, Louis, Liam and Niall, the official One Direction tour programme was produced to accompany the band on their first big concerts around the UK. The programme is pricey, as they tend to be, but for your money you get 24 pages, mainly packed with pictures of the boys!

tion Merchandise!

Official Poster
Various

A One Direction fan's wall isn't complete without a photo of the band on there somewhere – and the official One Direction store sells all sorts! You can get a poster of the band together, or individual posters of the boys are also available. Don't forget to use the posters in the middle of this Super-fan's guide, too!

Forever Young: Our Official X-Factory Story
£16.99

There's no shortage of pictures of the boys in the official book that was published a couple of months after they finished third in *The X-Factor* 2010. We're betting that you've probably already got the book, but in case you haven't, it charts the story of our fab five. It's got lots of pictures in it that you simply won't find anywhere else.

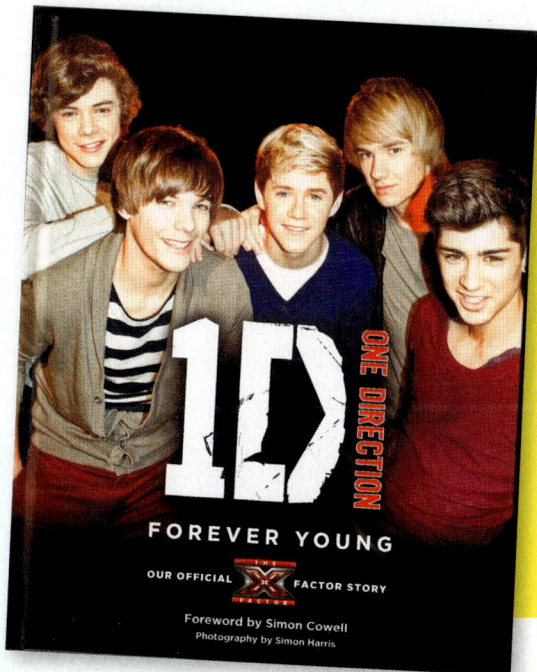

Dare To Dream: Life As One Direction
£16.99

Published to tie-in with the release of their first single, the second official book from One Direction digs even further into the back story of the boys. Once again, you get a whole bunch of previously unseen pictures, and there's lots of information about each of the band members individually. It's certainly worth a read!

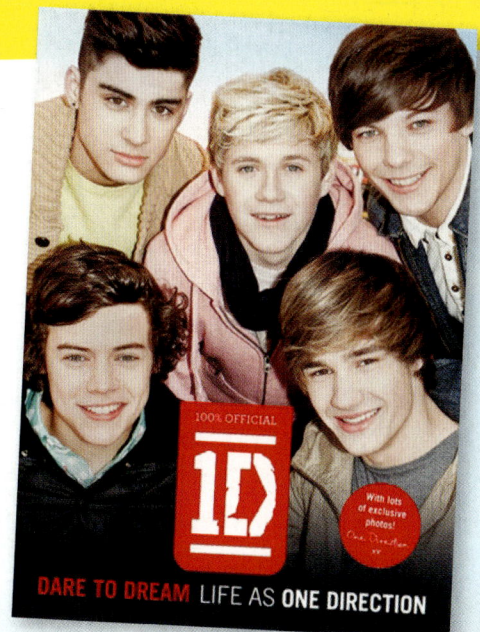

The One Direction Calendar!
Not in print anymore

There's a really, really good reason why the 2012 One Direction Calendar turned out to be one of the biggest sellers of all time... just check out the brilliant pictures of Niall, Louis, Liam, Zayn and Harry in it! It's unmissable, and it's selling for high prices on the second-hand market now that it's gone out of print.

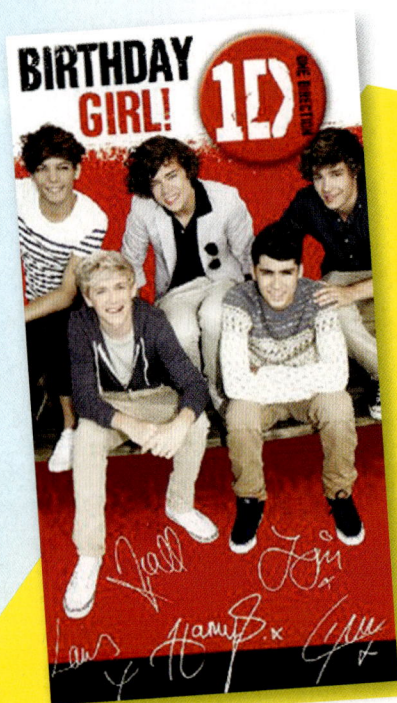

Official Greeting Cards!
Various

Which of us wouldn't want a member of One Direction for our birthday? Well, now we can! Sadly, it's just a picture of one of the boys, but still, the range of official One Direction greetings cards will get any birthday morning off to a good start. Plus, you can give them to all your friends, and spread the word about One Direction, too!

One Direction Clothes!
Various

If you head over to the official One Direction store – you can find it online at www.onedirectionstore.com – you'll find a wide selection of clothes, sporting the One Direction name. Some of them have pictures of the band on, too. We love the I Love One Direction T-shirts, as well as the special heart design pink hoodie. But which is your favourite?

6 Which member of One Direction had got to the later stages of *The X-Factor* in 2008?

7 True or false: amongst the products that One Direction endorse is Pokémon?

8 Which two members of One Direction live together?

9 On *The X-Factor*, who was One Direction's mentor?

10 Which member of One Direction comes from Doncaster?

11 Which member of One Direction was described as "the Irish Justin Bieber"?

12 In what category did One Direction win at the 2012 Brit Awards?

13 In which town was the *Up All Night* concert filmed for its DVD release?

14 Where did One Direction play the very first concert in their Up All Night Tour?

15 And where is the first gig in the 2013 World Tour?

16 Where did *Gotta Be You* get to in the UK singles chart?

17 How many tracks are there on the original release of the album, *Up All Night*?

18 Which record label released *Up All Night* in America?

19 What was the first UK number one single that One Direction sang on?

20 Whose audition for *The X-Factor* wasn't seen on the main show, but instead was screened for the first time on *The Xtra Factor*?

21 What was the name of the band that Harry was in before One Direction?

22 Had One Direction won *The X-Factor*, what would have been the name of the song they'd have released as their first single?

23 What does Niall describe as his best present ever, that he received at the age of 11?

24 Which member of the band briefly appears in the video for Ed Sheeran's song, *Drunk*?

25 Which member of the band is afraid of spoons?

Answers

1   Harry
2   Syco
3   Louis
4   Harry
5   Liam
6   Liam
7   True
8   Harry and Louis
9   Simon Cowell
10   Louis
11   Niall
12   Best British Single
13   Bournemouth
14   Watford
15   The O2 Arena, London
16   Number 3.
17   13
18   Columbia Records
19   Heroes, by The X-Factor Finalists
20   Zayn's
21   White Eskimo
22   Forever Young
23   A guitar
24   Harry
25   Liam

How Did You Do?

25
Wow! You are the ultimate One Direction Superfan!

20-24
You sure do love One Direction. You are one of the band's greatest fans!

14-19
Your One Direction knowledge is good, but there's a few more things ready for you to discover...

8-13
Hmmm, you need to swot up on your One Direction knowledge a little bit!

7 or under
You're a long way from being a Superfan, but it's going to be a lot of fun finding new things out about the boys!

Lots Of Things You Might Not Have Known About One Direction!

If you do a Google search for One Direction, you get over 1 billion results!

Google

Liam can apparently do an impression of Kermit The Frog!

Nickelodeon is interested in signing One Direction up for a TV show in the US!

Three big record labels in America wanted to sign up One Direction, but it was Columbia who eventually won!

One Direction appeared in an episode of the US TV show, iCarly!

Over 300,000 tickets for the UK leg of One Direction's 2013 World Tour were sold in one day!

2013
BUY YOUR TIC

The TV show Glee did a version of What Makes You Beautiful

153,965 copies of What Makes You Beautiful were sold in the UK in its first week on sale!

Harry once had a pet hamster, called Hamster!

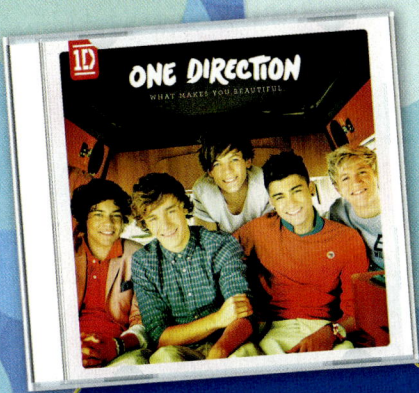

One Direction have apparently been invited to the White House!

If you follow them on Twitter, you know that One Direction are notorious for responding to the most random of Tweets!

One Direction were rumoured to be doing a record with Justin Bieber, but apparently it's not really happening

One Direction once performed a concert even though three of the boys were suffering from whiplash!

Harry can play the kazoo!

ONE DIRECTION
WHAT MAKES YOU BEAUTIFUL

RECTION

RLD TOUR
W BEFORE THEY SELL OUT!

One Direction got into trouble in New York for accidentally causing damage to a ten pin bowling alley!

Olly Murs supported One Direction as part of their 2012 American tour

Harry doesn't like beetroot!

Zayn has been expelled from school twice, both times for fighting

One Direction's calendar is the best-seller of all time at Amazon.com

A Directionater is the name given to someone who hates One Direction. The fools!

Up All Night sold 176,000 copies in its first week on sale in America!

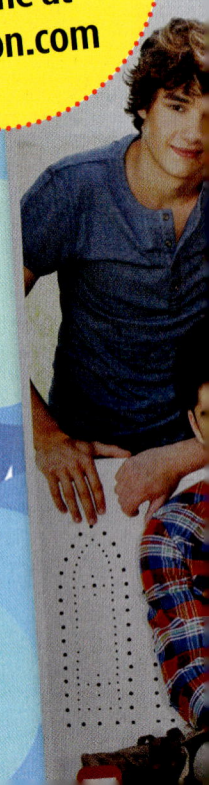

Rumours keep persisting that Harry has been offered solo work

Liam has revealed that his three sisters used to dress him up in their clothes!

You can see Harry in the music video for Ed Sheeran's Drunk

One Direction do promotional work for Pokémon!

On the way back from a gig in Birmingham, England, in January 2012, One Direction were involved in a traffic accident. Fortunately, everyone was okay!

Up All Night topped the iTunes charts within ten minutes of its release!

The boys have said that their next album will have more guitars, and be more grungey!

For an April Fool's joke, Louis tweeted that he was going to be a dad!

Liam has pet turtles!

ONE DIRECTION

L 2012 CALENDAR

Zayn has revealed that James Corden is One Direction's love guru!

The loudest cheers on the 2011 X-Factor Live Tour were reserved for One Direction!

Louis has criticised the fans who were horrible to his girlfriend online

Harry has four nipples!

One Direction have no intention of quitting Britain to go and live in America. Phew!

Simon Cowell banned Niall from dying his hair black!

JLS are rumoured to be unhappy at how One Direction have become so popular in the USA, whilst they haven't!

Harry has admitted that he loves being naked!

One Direction won't change their name, despite complaints from an American group with the same name

Niall likes girls who don't wear make-up

The boys reckon that Niall will be the first amongst them to get married

It seems that The Wanted are a bit jealous of One Direction's success, if the comments they keep making are anything to go by!

One Direction weren't allowed to turn on Christmas lights in UK cities last year, due to fears over crowd safety

The American release of Up All Night was brought forward, due to One Direction's popularity!

You can hire One Direction for your birthday party, but it would cost tens of thousands to do so!

Liam's sisters used to call him "Cheesy Head", because he used to eat so many cheesy crisps!

What's Next For One Direction?

Since they hit the big time, One Direction's schedule has taken the boys around the world, winning over millions of fans as they've gone on their incredible journey. In a short space of time, they've become household names, right across the planet!

But the One Direction story is only just beginning. Their success has been so stratospheric, it's easy to forget that the band only released their first single towards the end of 2011. We've had one album, a few singles, and lots and lots of happy memories. But there's so much more to come!

It all leads, of course, to the inevitable question: What will One Direction be doing next? Let's take a look...

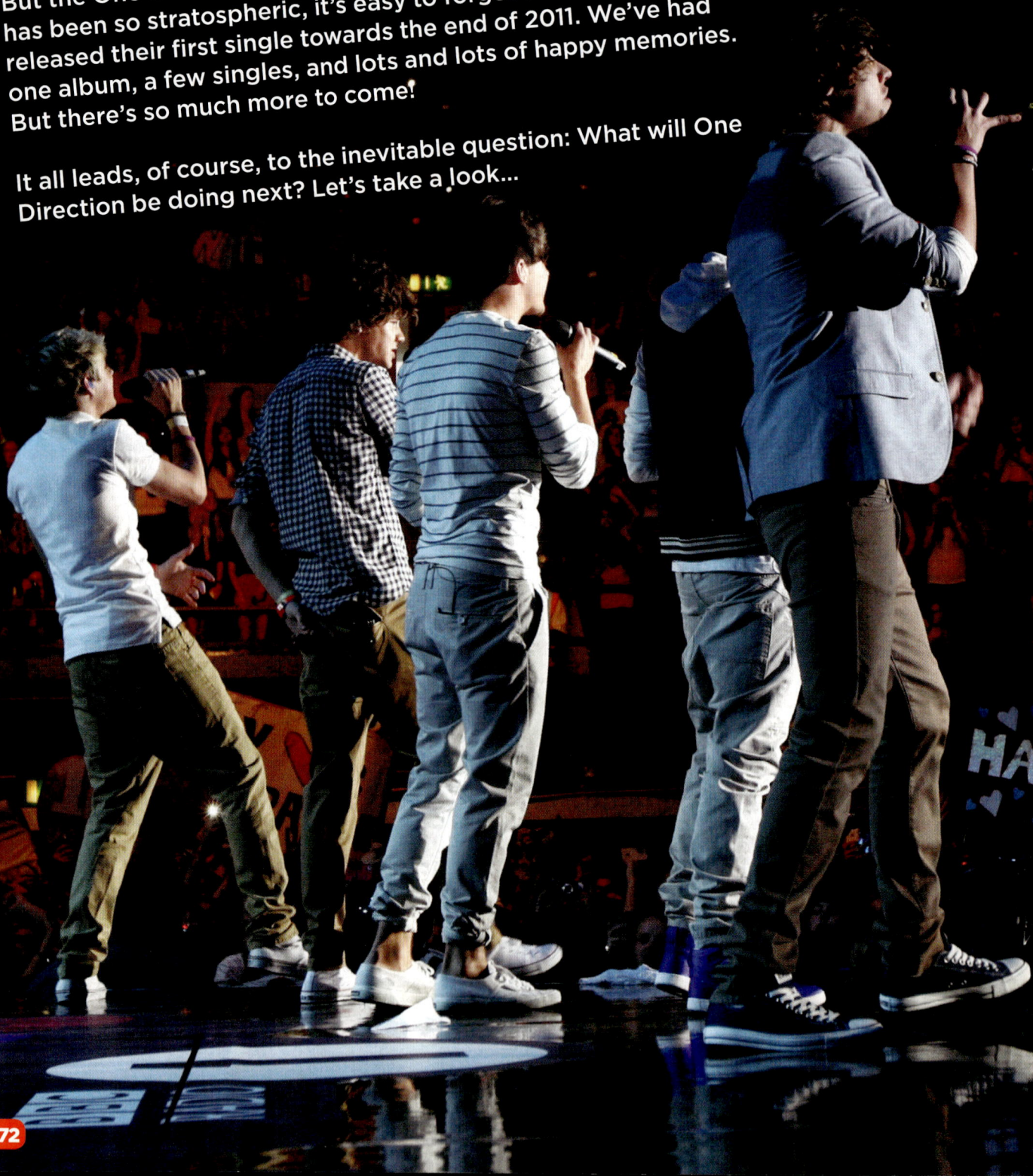

Music

The obvious first part of the answer is the massive world tour that the band has committed itself to. With hundreds of thousands of tickets sold in a matter of minutes, One Direction are set to travel to opposite ends of the globe with their new world tour.

But that doesn't mean that they won't be working on other projects. One Direction have already offered a few hints as to a second album. In February 2012, for instance, Louis told the *Daily Star* that "we want to take the next album into a different zone... more guitars and grungier".

The boys are potentially set to work with Ed Sheeran again on writing material and we know that they've already been recording new songs in Sweden! We'd hope the new album will be released late in 2013 or early in 2014, but maybe that's just us being hopeful.

Toys & Games

Elsewhere in the world of One Direction, there is more to look forward to. Hasbro, for instance, has announced that it's going to be releasing a load of One Direction toys and games, as well as figures of each of the boys. That's got to be something to look forward to!

Film & TV Show

There's also been rumours of a One Direction movie doing the rounds, too. Apparently, if it goes ahead, it'd be a film that tells the story of how they came together on *The X-Factor*, and went from that point onwards to world stardom. It's more likely to be a documentary-style film than anything else, and we await any further details with keen interest.

There's also talk of a One Direction television show, too. The boys have already popped up on a few different TV shows (including a brief appearance on iCarly!) and might be signed up in America by Nickelodeon to develop their own television programme!

Nickelodeon has confirmed that the project is in the works, although there's still some way to go before it makes it to our screens. The boys have denied that it's happening a few times, but we sincerely hope they're just fibbing!

Bright Future

One thing's for sure. The future is bright and rosey for the boys of One Direction, and we hope that they'll keep making music together for a long, long time to come.

Once they've finished their 2013 world tour, they're going to have a lot of projects to choose from, and we can't wait to see what they get up to next!

Awards & Milestones

They've only been together for a year or two, but already One Direction have some significant achievements under their belts...

2010

The X-Factor: 3rd Place

2011

First single goes to number 1

First album goes to number 2

4 Music Awards: Best Group

4 Music Awards: Best Breakthrough

4 Music Awards: Best Video

J-14 Teen Icon Awards: Icon Of Tomorrow

US Gold Record: Up All Night

US Platinum Single: What Makes You Beautiful

2012

The Brit Awards: Best British Single

UK Kids' Choice Awards: Favourite UK Newcomer

UK Kids' Choice Awards: Favourite UK Band

World arena tour announced, sells at record speed